Goldfish

Goldfish

B. Ahilan
N. Felix
Associate Professors
Department of Aquaculture
Fisheries College & Research Institute,
Tamilnadu Veterinary and Animal Sciences University,
Thoothukudi - 628 008, T.N
&
J.D. Jameson
Director of Research and Extension (Fisheries),
Tamilnadu Veterinary and Animal Sciences University,
Chennai

2009
DAYA PUBLISHING HOUSE
Delhi - 110 035

ISBN 81-7035-603-2
ISBN 978-81-7035-603-5

Published by : **Daya Publishing House**
1123/74, Deva Ram Park
Tri Nagar, Delhi - 110 035
Phone: 27383999
Fax: (011) 23260116
e-mail : dayabooks@vsnl.com
website : www.dayabooks.com

Showroom : 4760-61/23, Ansari Road, Darya Ganj,
New Delhi - 110 002
Phone: 23245578, 23244987

Laser Typesetting : **Classic Computer Services**
Delhi - 110 035

Printed at : **Chawla Offset Printers**
Delhi - 110 052

PRINTED IN INDIA

TAMIL NADU VETERINARY AND ANIMAL SCIENCES UNIVERSITY
Madhavaram Milk Colony
Chennai–600 051

Foreword

Aquaculture has emerged as one of the growing food producing sectors in the world. Like aquaculture, ornamental fish culture has earned reputation in this century world wide as trade as well as industry. As a network fisheries enterprise, this sector is serving as a source of self-employment to millions of people. In Singapore and Malaysia, ornamental fish trade has become a big bizarre and playing a significant role in the economy and making opportunity for other developing and developed countries. Day by day newer fish species are added and technologies developed for the captive breeding of a number of native and exotic varieties. In Tamil Nadu, Chennai contributes much to this trade like other cosmopolitan cities.

India being a tropical country, many species of ornamental fishes are bred and exported to other countries. Tamil Nadu's ornamental fish trade is gaining momentum due to conducive environment and technical manpower. The pet fish 'goldfish' is one among the popular aquarium fishes having good market potential in the country and abroad. Hobbyists, students, researchers and entrepreneurs have to learn much about the biology and behaviour of this important fish species. There is no comprehensive publication on Goldfish for use as textbook by the students, researchers and fish culturists. As the book on Goldfish emphasizes more on the biology, culture and breeding aspects, it could cater to the needs of the aquarium traders also.

I appreciate the effort of the authors for bringing out an exclusive book on goldfish with detailed information for the benefit of fishery sectors.

Dr. P. Thangaraju, *Ph.D.,*
Vice-chancellor
TANUVAS,
Chennai

Preface

A number of publications on Aquarium keeping are available from many countries. But in India, where ornamental fish culture is now being popularized, publication on the most important ornamental fish variety Goldfish with reference to our agro-climatic conditions are lacking. In order to fill up this long-felt gap, the present work has been taken up.

A wide range of aspects of goldfish such as, history of goldfish, anatomy, species and varieties of goldfish, selection and transportation, Goldfish culture in aquarium and pond, care to be taken for goldfish, preparation of feed and feeding management, breeding aspects of goldfish, health care and economics and marketing aspects of goldfish have been dealt with. It is hoped that this contribution presented in an easy to read style with a number of photographs would be of great use to all students who have fisheries in their curriculum and also a standard guide for the researches and entrepreneurs.

We are highly indebted to Dr. P. Thangaraju, *Ph.D.*, Vice-Chancellor, Tamil Nadu Veterinary and Animal Sciences University, Chennai for his Foreword. We are thankful to Dr. V.K. Venkataramani, *Ph.D.*, Dean, Fisheries College and Research Institute for his kind help in the preparation of this publication. We extend our thanks to Mr. Chermaraj for his secretarial assistance.

Authors

Contents

Chapter 1
Introduction

The carp family is the largest of the fish families; the *Cyprinidae* comprise around two thousand species and occupy most of the world's water. The carp family initially originated in East Asia and subsequently spreaded to the rest of Eurasia, Africa and North America. Both *Cyprinus* and *Carassius* followed this course of migration and these carps have made their way across Asia and into Europe. It is important to note that the goldfish is a distinct species; it is not, as has been claimed, a variation of the Crucian carp. The goldfish was one of the earliest fish to be domesticated and still one of the most commonly kept aquarium fish.

The History and Development of the Goldfish

The date that the first goldfish reached Japan is also somewhat indefinite; however, it is reasonably certain that by 1500 AD, they had become established in that country. The Japanese icthyologist, Mitsukuri wrote in 1904 that there was a record of about 1500, in which it was noted that some goldfish had been taken from China to Sakai, near Osaka, Japan. It seems that two centuries were to elapse before the Japanese began breeding goldfish–the honour of being the first to breed the goldfish in Japan is accorded to Sato Sanzaemon of Koriyama, during the Hoyei era of 1704-1710.

By the end of the seventeenth century, the goldfish had become wide-spread throughout the East. About 1750, goldfish arrived at the French port of Lorient. They were imported by the French East-India Company during the last days of the French monarchy. By 1754 the goldfish had reached the Netherlands it had already become known in Italy where they were placed into ponds.

By the end of the eighteenth century the goldfish was flourishing in the Russian climate. Available records show the goldfish arrived in America in 1874.

From these original importations, and the mutations, the Japanese goldfish breeders have produced many varieties that have become well known to Western goldfish enthusiasts. Probably the best known of all being the Lionhead. There is absolutely no doubt the true Lionhead was developed by the Japanese in the nineteenth century.

There are two basic types of goldfish–"scaled" and "scaleless". The scaled fishes are the common goldfish, comets, fantails, and others. The irregular spots of black, white, and gold appear, and in a few more weeks the black and white disappears, and the fish are covered with opaque, red-gold scales, bright and metallic. The so-called scaleless fish actually have transparent scales which look like a delicate skin. This makes beautiful glowing, but not shining, colours possible among forms like the Shubunkins and

Calicos. Their colours, including blues and lavenders, appear in many combinations.

Classification of the Goldfish

Kingdom	Animalia
Phylum	Chordata
Sub-phylum	Vertebrata
Class	Osteichthyes
Sub-class	Actinopterygii
Infra-class	Teleostei
Super-order	Ostariophysi
Order	Cypriniformes
Family	Cyprinidae
Sub-family	Cyprininae
Genus	Carassius
Species	*auratus*

The true carps are characterized by a long dorsal fin, which covers approximately half the length of the dorsal contour form the snout to the tip of the caudal peduncle. The common carp is characterized by the possession of two pairs of barbels, which are absent in all members of the genus *Carassius*. The crucian carp (*Carassius carassius*) has a characteristically deeper body than the goldfish, with 7-9 scales from the base of the dorsal spine to the lateral line, compared with 5-6 in the case of the goldfish. The number of scales along the length of the lateral line is greater in the crucian carp than in the goldfish: 28-35 as against 25-30. This difference is partly related to the somewhat larger size of scales in the goldfish *via-a-vis* the crucian carp.

The body form is relatively long and laterally compressed. The dorsal and ventral contours from the snout to the caudal peduncle are smooth. The body width is approximately two-thirds of its depth. Depth of body and length of the head are each about one-third of the body length. The lateral line describes a slightly sigmoid curve, forming an almost horizontal straight line. The height of the dorsal fin and the length of the pectoral, pelvic and anal fins are very similar and one-sixth of the body length generally. The dorsal and ventral lobes of the caudal fin are equal in length; the indentation of its trailing edge may be half the length of the lobes. Lobe length is around a quarter of the body length.

In order to understand colouration of goldfish it is required to know how it is actually produced. In the goldfish there are three colour components, namely melanin which produces the darker components of colour, black, brown, blue and grey, the xanthic pigments which produce red, orange and yellow shades, and finally guanine which in the absence of the other two pigment types gives a white or silvery colour. Generally, the guanine, when deposited on the scales, give them a metallic sheen. If scales are transparent, guanine deposited in the dermis produces a mother-of-pearl or nacreous sheen. In the absence of melanin, xanthic pigments and guanine the body shows a pink tinge which is due to blood haemoglobin in superficial capillary blood vessels.

When it was found that goldfish could be kept more or less indefinitely in good health in relatively small containers then the goldfish was poised to become the pet of the masses, which subsequently came to pass not only in China but elsewhere in the world. Goldfish may grow to a maximum length of 53 cm and a maximum weight of 4.5 kg. In optimal condition goldfish may live more than 20 years but most goldfish in aquaria generally live only for 6-8 years. A group of goldfish is known as a troubling.

Diversification

The development and evolution of new variants of goldfish is still continuing, mainly in China. Many of these in essence are ringing changes on established themes, but it is hoped that through a better understanding and application of genetic principles we can more easily conserve and maintain the diversity of goldfish forms and also augment for future reference as for study the evolutionary sequence.

Chapter 2
Anatomy of the Goldfish

Scales

Goldfish scales are evenly curved, smooth and flexible. When the newly hatched fish first emerges from the egg it is totally devoid of scales. Within a short time, however, minute scales appear in the skin and form a complete covering by the time the fish has grown to 13 mm in length. The number of scales will remain constant in its life-time. No further scales will develop except for replacement. Fish scales are dead material, similar to the human finger nail. Each scale is composed of two layers: a flexible, fibrous lower layer, and an upper brittle layer formed by a deposit of clear bony dentine. As the fish grows, the scales must also grow in order to continue to overlap the scales behind them. This is done by the individual scale adding new rings of dentine around its edge, in much the same way that a tree grows. The scales, which are transparent, are bedded in the dermis and provide protection to the body of the fish, covering the fish from behind the gill-covers to the root of the tail. Scales are absent from the head which is bare.

Skin and Pigmentation

The skin is composed of two layers: the thin, cellular, outer epidermis, and the inner dermis which is composed of connective tissue. The epidermis covers the head and body-scales of the fish, it produces a mucus–it is this which makes the fish feel slimy to the touch–the secretion acting as a protection against diseases and parasites, and it also reduces friction. Beneath the dermis there is a layer of fat (adipose tissue) and muscle (myotomes).

The dermis contains a substance called guanine–a reflective substance that lies just under the scales and also at a lower depth. This light, reflective substance is a white material which collects in clusters of crystals known as iridocytes.

In addition to the iridocytes, the dermis—and to an extend the epidermis–contains colour pigment cells known as chromatophores, these being disposed at different depths within the tissue. These pigments may be red-orange, yellow or black (the pigments are the same in all fish, no other pigments having been discovered). The red-orange and yellow pigments, known as lipochromes, are liquid, while the black are called melamines. The pigments are relatively large cells of irregular, ramified shape, containing the colour-matter inside themselves in the form of droplets or grainlets. They are capable of concentrating all the pigment into a tiny spot in the centre of each cell, or of expanding it out all over the cell. It is possible for some cells to expand at the same moment that others are contracting.

All varieties of goldfish, no matter what shape they may be, can normally be placed in one of three groups–Metallic, Nacreous or Matt–depending on the amount and disposition of the reflective tissue.

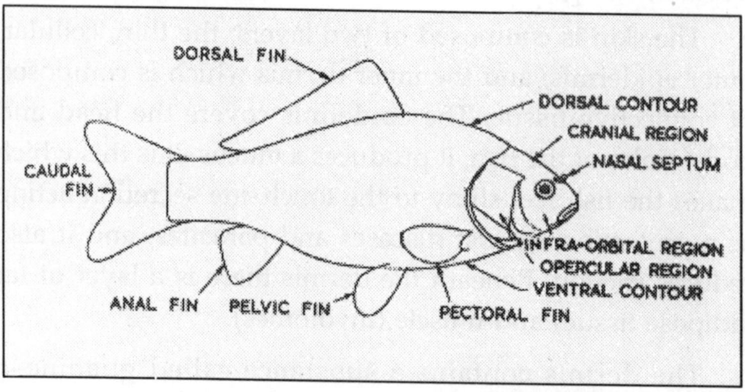

Figure 1: Goldfish Finnage and Body Plan

Metallic Group

This group has a metallic shine due to there being normal placement of the iridocytes, giving full reflection over the head and body.

Nacreous

In this group most areas lack the upper layer of iridocytes allowing the deeper layer to show. This lower layer of reflective tissue appears as a mother-of-pearl shine (nacreous). The individual fish therefore exhibits a nacreous shine and, possibly, a few scales with metallic shine; these scales should be as few as possible.

Matt

An absolute lack of shine, due to a complete absence of reflective iridocytes, is the mark of fish in this group. All regions of the head and body have a matt appearance.

Colour

The pigments in goldfish are red-orange, yellow and black. The red-orange and yellow pigments are found in the epidermis and the dermis—the red and orange tending to be in the area just below the scales, while the yellow is just above the scales. The black pigment is found in the epidermis, dermis, adipose tissue and myotomes. In the upper region the pigment appears black, in the next lower it is slate-blue, in the adipose tissue it is a bright blue, and in the lowest layer of tissue it shows as a brilliant blue.

Haemoglobin is responsible for the pink body colour of most matt fish and some nacreous fish; it is also responsible for the deep red colour of the gills of matt and some nacreous fish. This red is due to the concentration of blood in the gills showing through the translucent bones of the opercula. Due to the pigments lying at differing depths it is possible for them to overlap and thereby create a variety of colours other than those of the pigments.

The Metallic group of goldfish may be reddish-orange or yellow. In the absence of pigment, they will be silver; due to the reflective whitish tissue showing through the transparent scales. Within this group, also, are wild olive coloured types (these are fish which have not changed to the reddish-orange or yellow colour, and is due to black pigment combined with the other pigments). The young of this group, when first scaled, are olive in colour, after a time this darkens to almost black. As the fish develops the black will begin to recede deeper into the tissues, and as it does so the other pigments will be revealed. Eventually the black pigment will be so deep in the tissues that it cannot be seen. During this colour change the fish may be reddish-orange, yellow, silver and black–that is an extreme example of multi-colouration in the metallic group–but more often it is a single colour plus a non-permanent black.

The Matt group are usually pink with black eyes, but it is possible to find fish with colours similar to those in the next group. Due to the lack of reflective tissues the intensity of colours will appear different.

The Nacreous group, being the most colourful, may exhibit either a single colour or a number of different colours as follows: whitish-pink, yellow, orange, red, blue, violet, brown and black, and any multiplicity of those colours.

Chapter 3
Species and Varieties of Goldfish

Selective breeding over centuries has produced several colour variations, some of them far removed from the "golden" colour of the originally domesticated fish. Goldfish may also lose their "golden" colour, or rather any goldfish colour, by being kept in a dark room, this causes the scales to turn white. There are also different body shapes, fin and eye configurations.

Common Goldfish

The common goldfish, *Carassius auratus* is the patriarchs of ornamental fish varieties for excepting the tropicals. These are the fish from which most of the fancy breeds have been developed. The common goldfish is hardier than most of its descendants, remains healthy under a wider range of water temperatures, and will even survive a few hours out of water, if kept moist. It breeds prolifically, and it eats

Figure 2: Common Goldfish

practically anything. It is a favorite for its hardy nature and can be trained to eat from the hand.

Body

Elongated, laterally compressed, depth 3/7–3/8 body length.

Fins

Dorsal and anal fins single, pectoral and pelvics paired. Caudal fin single, spread approximately equal to body depth, lobes approximately 1/4 body length with somewhat rounded ends. Doral fin about 3/8 body depth.

Eyes

Normal

Contours

Smooth with approximately equal dorsal and ventral curvature, smooth lateral contours.

Colouration

Metallic, red, orange, yellow, blue, brown, black, silver, self-colours and variegated. Fins have same colour as body or contrasting.

Comet

The Comet was developed in the late 1880's, first by accident and later by selective breeding. The body is more elongated and there is much more elaborate fin and tail development than in the parent. The extensive fins and tail make the Comet one of the fastest and most graceful of all goldfish. It swims with smooth, darting movements often too fast for the eye to follow.

Body

Elongated, laterally compressed, depth approximately 1/3 body length.

Fins

Dorsal and anal fins single, pectorals and pelvics paired, caudal fin, long equal in length to that of the body or longer,

Figure 3: Comet

held well spread. Fins and lobes long, narrow and pointed, dorsal as deep or deeper than body.

Eyes

Normal

Contours

Smooth with approximately equal dorsal and ventral curvature, smooth lateral contours.

Colouration

Commonly red, orange or red and with variegated, other metallic colours possible. Fins are of the same colour as body or contrasting.

Fantail

Another strain of the common goldfish is the fantail, whose movements are slow and deliberate. A single instead of a double anal fin is also considered undesirable. The body is shorter with a tendency to become egg-shaped and the fins are appreciably longer. The fantail is a deservedly popular fish and it is colourful and hardy, suitable for both

Figure 4: Fantail

aquarium and pond. It occurs in metallic and calico forms, the metallics are probably somewhat hardier.

Body

Short, globular, depth greater than 3/5 body length.

Fins

Dorsal fin is single, anals, pectorals and pelvics are paired, caudal is double, bifurcated held without dropping below horizontal, spread up to 1.5 times body depth, length of caudal half body length with rounded lobes, dorsal 1/3–1/2 body length.

Eyes

Normal

Contours

Smooth dorsal, ventral and lateral contours.

Colouration

Both metallic and calico forms are produced.

Veiltail

The body is shorter and chunkier than that of the Fantail, and fins and tail grow so long they drape gracefully in filmy folds, far out of proportion to the size of the body. It takes two years, or longer, for the Veiltail to reach full development and beauty, and once it does, feeding must be watched closely. If fed too much, fins and tail will continue to develop, becoming thick, and finally split and ragged.

Body

Short and globular, depth 3/4 or more body length.

Figure 5: Veiltail

Fins

Dorsal fin single, anals, pectorals and pelvics paired, caudal fin double with straight-cut trailing edge, very broad with a downward carriage, length 3/4–1.5 times body length. The dorsal fin should equal or exceed the body depth.

Eyes

Normal

Contours

Dorsal contour smooth without a hump, ventral and lateral contours smooth.

Shubunkin

Shubunkin is comparatively a newcomer, introduced by the Japanese about the beginning of this century. It is a scaleless hybrid, one parent being the common goldfish, the other a Demekin, a pop-eyed fish with scales usually uniform black, pale-red, or pale reddish-yellow, but

Figure 6: Shubunkin

sometimes variegated. In form and size, the Shubunkin resembles the common goldfish, the colouring usually in patches of red, black, blue, yellow, brown, and lavender upon a pearl or pale-blue background, but often bright-red Shubunkins, attractively spotted black, will show up. On rare occasions a new brood may contain shubunkins which are uniformly purple or lavender. Like the common goldfish, the Shubunkin is hardy and quite active in either pool or aquarium.

Body

Elongated, laterally compressed, depth 3/7-3/8 body length.

Fins

Dorsal and anal fins single, pectorals and pelvics paired in all, caudal single, spread approximately equal to body depth, lobes approximately 1/4 body length with rounded ends, fins of same size as in the common goldfish.

Eyes

Normal

Contours

Smooth dorsal and ventral contours as in common goldfish.

Colouration

Calico colours and pattern, blue background with patches of red, orange and yellow overlaid with even pattern of dark brown or black spots and patches. These features are associated with transparent scales.

Telescope Eye

The name telescope-eye has been used for well over a century to describe the protuberant eyes of some goldfish. The condition of exophthalmia which the telescope eye shows can occur in nature as a pathological condition but in the goldfish the cause is genetic and is produced by a simple gene mutation. The feature is virtually confined to short-bodied fish but fish with telescope eyes collectively

Figure 7: Telescope Eye

show an enormous range of variation. The shape of the eye varies, it may be spherical, ovoid, a truncated cone or a segmented sphere.

Body

Short and globular, depth 3/4 or more body length.

Fins

Dorsal fin single, anals, pectorals and pelvics paired, caudal fin double with variable length. In butterfly-tails caudals are held with a near horizontal spread.

Eyes

Protuberant, may be spherical, segmented, ovoid or in the form of a truncated cone.

Contours

Smooth dorsal, ventral and lateral contours, a Ryukin-like hump may develop in some individuals.

Colouration

A remarkable variety of colours are developed, mostly metallics although calicos are known, black is most popular, variegated black and white or red forms have also been produced.

Lionhead

A strange and beautiful fish, the smooth, humped back, nearly globular body, and no dorsal fin. This makes it an extremely poor swimmer. Unable to maintain balance, it often swims upside down or vertically with head down. It is the head growth which gives the Lionhead its name. It is also called Buffalohead, which is even more descriptive of the shape of the odd growth.

Figure 8: Lionhead

The malformation on the head beings to take shape fairly late in the first year and becomes larger and longer. As the fish ages, the growth begins to form thickly over the gill plates, which makes breathing difficult.

The Lionhead will then seek cooler water which is well oxygenated. Even in the best surrounding possible, the fish may suddenly die, presumably of suffocation. Some Lionheads fail to develop the head growth, and these remain quite hardy.

Body

Short and globular, two types: Ranchu with strongly curved back, Chinese Lionhead with a straighter back, body depth 5/8–3/4 length.

Fins

Dorsal fin absent, anals, pectorals and pelvics double, caudal fin double, forked with no downward sweep, 1/4–3/8 of body length.

Eyes

Normal.

Contours

Dorsal contour depends on extent of the variable hood development, otherwise dorsal, ventral and lateral contours should be smooth.

Colouration

A wide range of metallic colours are found and calico, colours variegated or self, body and hood colours similar or contrasting, redcaps etc., hoods may be bi- or multicoloured.

Celestial

This is a remarkable fish, with a body shaped like that of the Chinese Telescope. The colouring is a uniform black or pale orange, or a combination of the two in mottled pattern. Most striking is the eye formation, the pupils being situated on top of the eyeballs, so that the fish seems to be gazing heavenward—hence the name Celestial. The absence of the dorsal fin is a characteristic feature of the Celestial. The Celestial is a metallic fish commonly red-orange or red and white in colour. Individuals with strongly

Figure 9: Celestial

contrasting coloured fins can be very striking, such as black fins against a red body or red fins with a silver body. The Chinese have recently produced a Celestial with a dorsal fin.

Body

Short and globular or medium length and less globular, depth 1/2–3/4 body length.

Fins

Dorsal absent, anals, pectorals and pelvics paired, medium-short in length, caudal fin double 3/8–1/2 body length, bifurcated.

Eyes

Large, protuberant, upwardly directed.

Contours

Dorsal, ventral and lateral contours smooth.

Colouration

Common metallic colours and calicoes are found.

Bubble-eye

In its general body conformation the Bubble-eye is basically similar to the Celestial and has finnage of similar length. The bubbles are produced by the growth of large vesicles arising from the lower orbit; their growth frequently causes displacement of the eye so that the iris faces upwards as in the Celestial. Close examination shows that the eye itself is not in fact enlarged in the majority of such fish.

The usual metallic colours are to be seen in Bubble-eyes-reds, red and white, orange and black.

Figure 2: Common Goldfish
(Page 12)

Figure 3: Comet
(Page 13)

Figure 4: Fantail (Page 14)

Figure 5: Veiltail (Page 16)

Figure 7: Telescope Eye
(Page 18)

Figure 6: Shubunkin (Page 17)

Figure 8: Lionhead (Page 20)

Figure 9: Celestial (Page 21)

Figure 11: Pearl-scale (Page 24)

Figure 10: Bubble-eye (Page 23)

Figure 12: Oranda (Page 25)

Figure 13: Black Moor (Page 26)

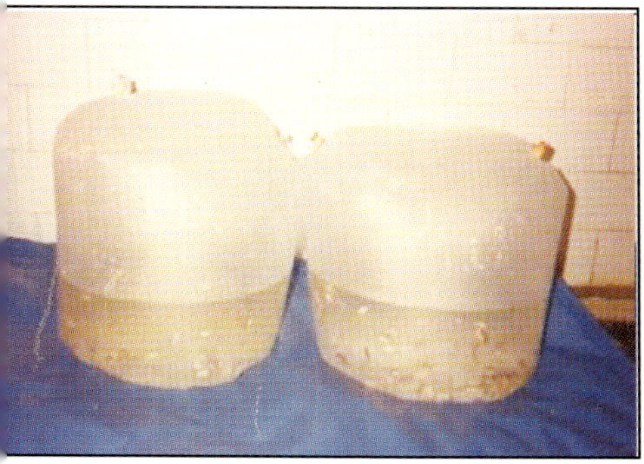

Figure 14: Oxygen Packed Fishes in Polythene Bag (Page 31)

Figure 15: All Glass Tank (Page 33)

Figure 16: Ornamental Fish Culture Ponds (Page 36)

Figure 17: Artificial Feed (Page 50)

Figure 18: Live Food Organisms (Page 51)

Figure 19: Watering in the Cement Cistern (Page 57)

Figure 20: Introducing Aquatic Weed (Page 58)

Figure 21: Introducing the Fishes (Page 59)

Figure 22: . Feeding the Fishes (Page 59)

Figure 10: Bubble-eye

Body

Short and globular or medium length and less globular, depth 1/2–3/4 body length.

Fins

Dorsal absent, anals, pectorals and pelvics paired, medium-short in length, caudal fin double 3/8–1/2 body length, bifurcated.

Eyes

Characteristic 'water bubble-eye' developed, an infraorbital vesicle, eye may be displaced with iris directed upwards.

Contours

Dorsal, ventral and lateral contours smooth.

Colouration

Common metallic colours and calicoes are found.

Pearl-scale

The Pearl-scale is a very distinctive variety characterized by the eponymous scale which is convex rather than flat with a conspicuous centrally placed boss–the pearl. The body proportions in relation to the finnage are basically those of the Fantail; however, the body characteristically is very globose, almost as though the fish was dropsical. The caudal fins are usually indented but variants occur where this is straight-cut and the fins generally are longer.

The Pearl-scale is found in a range of metallic forms in addition to the calico. The original form is very appealing and attractive and it would be worthwhile to take appropriate steps to safeguard its future.

Body

Short and extremely globular, body depth greater than 2/3 length, carries characteristic domed scales.

Figure 11: Pearl-scale

Fins

Dorsal single, anals, pectorals and pelvics double, caudal fin double, variable in shape, forked or square-cut, and in length 1/2 that of body or longer.

Eyes

Normal.

Contours

Dorsal, ventral and lateral contours smooth, the trunk is almost circular viewed from above.

Colouration

A wide range of colours are produced, both metallic and calico.

Oranda

This is a modification of the Lionhead and far superior to it, although the colouring of the two is similar. The shape of the Oranda tends more toward that of the veiltail, including tail and fin development. There is a dorsal fin. The head growth is also modified, being confined principally to the top of the head. It does not spread so as to hamper the fish. This is a comparatively fragile fish which does best in aquariums.

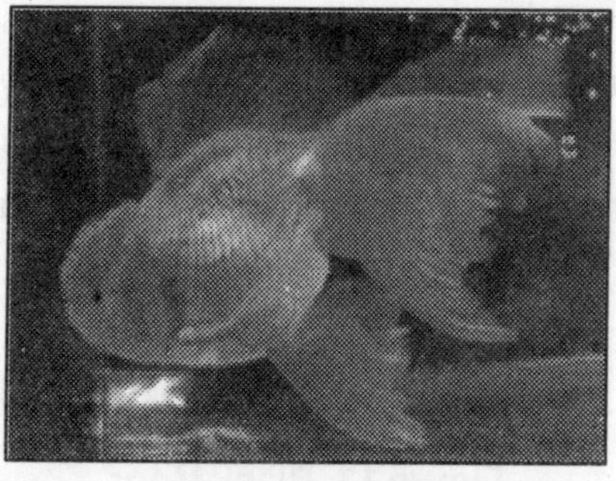

Figure 12: Oranda

Body

Short and globular, depth 2/3 or more of body length.

Fins

Dorsal single, anals, pectorals and pelvics double, caudal fin double, forked or broadtail with a downward sweep, 3/4-1.5 times body length, dorsal fin 1/2–7/8 body depth.

Eyes

Normal.

Contours

Characteristic hood in head region, otherwise smooth dorsal, ventral and lateral contours.

Colouration

Wide range of metallic colours and calico, variegated and self-colours, contrasting colouration of hood and body, redcap, bicoloured and multicoloured hoods can develop.

Black Moor

An extremely pretty fish, on the small side, usually a sooty, velvety black, and of short, chunky telescope form. Although most popular as blacks, pale-red and pale reddish-

Figure 13: Black Moor

yellow Moors do occur now and then. A uniformly black Moor may shade off to blue-gray or a golden cast along the underside of the belly. Those with blue-gray casts usually retain their black colour. Those with a golden cast sometimes turn gold. The Moor is a tricky fish to breed, especially with a good black colouring in mind. The best black offspring come not from two black parents.

Chapter 4
Selection and Transportation

Selecting Healthy Fish

Care and attention should be given to the selection of goldfish that is to be purchased. Careful observation and a sharp eye can help to reduce the risk of buying a sick or ailing fish. Patience and discretion will pay dividends by lessening the risk of buying a sick one and wasting money.

A close inspection of the tanks will reveal whether the dealer is concerned for the welfare of the stock. The tanks should be spacious and clean, without undue overcrowding of the fish. The fish should appear active, not sulking, with no dead fish in evidence. If all seems well, greater attention can be paid to the condition of the fish. They should be swimming actively without any difficulty or jerkiness. The eyes should be clear and bright with no trace of a cloudy, whitish film. The fins held erect and well spread should be free of any milkiness or blood streaks. The body must appear to be well nourished and have no sign of injury or disease.

Dull cloudy eyes, or eyes covered by a whitish film; split or torn fins; blood spots or streaks upon the body or fins; a grayish-white bloom or film that partially obscures the colour on any part of the body or head; scales that seem to be raised instead of lying flat. Any traces of small white 'cotton-wool' tufts of fungus, any minute white spot, pimples, ulcers, or holes, and apparent pieces of 'thread' anywhere on the fish. These are all positive signs of future trouble and such fish must be avoided.

Treatment of Newly-acquired Fish

Having chosen the fish, fill the carrying bucket about half full with some of the water from the tank in which it has been living, and gently place the fish into it. Transport the fish home as quickly as possible to avoid it depleting the oxygen in the water, although it may well take a considerable time before the fish suffers any ill-effects. It is possible to buy small battery-operated air-pumps, which would be very useful if the journey was likely to be excessively long. Aeration could be supplied to the water for a short spell every hour or so, allowing safe carriage of the fish for many hours–possibly days–without the fish suffering from lack of oxygen. Food is not necessary; a healthy goldfish can go without food for a number of days if need be, and feeding would only cause possible fouling of the water.

Upon arriving home it should be placed in the previously prepared container for an hour or two, to allow the temperatures to equalize. After sufficient time has elapsed, some of the water from the bucket can be poured into container. Ideally, the mixture of the waters should be very approximately fifty per cent of each. This is to give the fish as little shock as possible if the characters of the waters are very different. The fish can then be very gently placed into the receiving tank, where it should be left for around twenty-eight days. During this period partial changes of water should be made to help the fish adjust to the new water conditions, always making sure that there is no great variation in the water temperatures. Throughout this period of acclimatization a careful watch must be kept for any sign of disease and appropriate action should be taken if any symptoms appear. Two weeks are usually long enough for any dormant disease to break out, if the fish has the misfortune to be carrying any. While the fish is in the holding tank, it is a wise precaution to give it one or two disinfectant baths against flukes, with a final bath prior to being placed into its permanent home.

During the isolation period, the fish should be fed sparingly, commencing with very small feeds and gradually increasing the amounts offered. Normally fish purchased from a commercial source have been fed very frugally and are somewhat starved. The strength and appetite of the fish must be built up slowly by offering good nourishing types of foods, a little at a time. There may be times when a newly acquired fish is so starved, or perhaps suffering from severe stress, that it may show no inclination to accept dried foods. In that case gently aerate the water and offer a little live food, such as daphnia. This may well revive the fish's interest–for most fish are attracted to moving food. Additionally, such a fish should be kept quiet and interfered with as little as possible until it has recovered and commenced to feed normally.

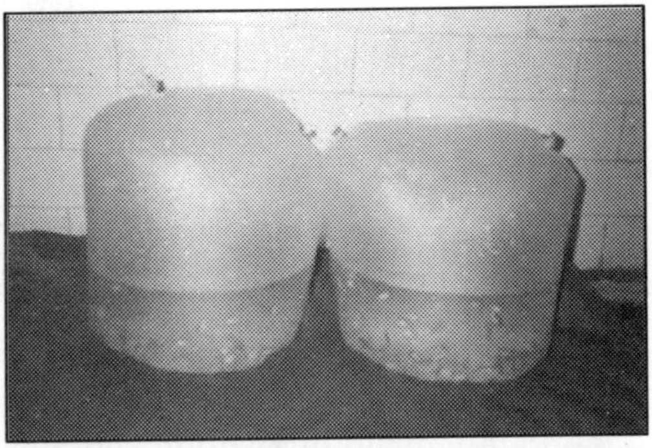

Figure 14: Oxygen Packed Fishes in Polythene Bag

At the end of quarantine period, the fish has proved itself healthy, it may be placed into an aquarium or pond. The easiest method of making the transfer is to place the fish and its water into a bucket which can then be floated in the water of the new home until the temperatures have equalized. If the container is gently tipped onto its side, the fish will swim out. On no account fish should be thrown into the water; such action will shock the fish. It could result in the loss of the fish, or at least cause the fish to develop air-bladder trouble.

Chapter 5
Fish Keeping in Aquarium and Pond

Setting-up the Aquarium

The appearance of the tank is very important. It should be cleaned thoroughly making sure that all smudges and smears are removed and dried to a sparkling clarity. The all-glass tank must have a layer of expanded polystyrene placed between the stand and the tank to prevent damage. If 'under-gravel' filtration is to be employed the unit should be installed at this stage. The perforated plates, or tubes are to be placed to cover the bottom of the tank. The amount of flexible plastic tubing required to reach from the filter to the air-pump should be measured and cut into required length and connected to the air-lift of the filter.

The gravel should be cleaned and placed it spread evenly over the base, building up gradually to a depth of 2–3 inches at the back and sloping gently down to the front.

Figure 15: All Glass Tank

Filling the tank is not merely a case of pouring water onto the gravel. First the gravel should be covered with a sheet of newspaper, upon this stand a deep plate. Water can now be slowly poured into the plate from where it will overflow onto the paper and, provided the water is not poured too fast, the paper will prevent the water disturbing the gravel. As the level of the water rises the paper may float up around the plate but it will still protect the gravel. When the tank is sufficiently full, the plate can be removed, and the paper slowly and carefully slid out of the water. The tank should be allowed to stand for a day after which a hose pipe can be used to remove about fifty per cent of the water, at the same time gentle siphoning out any sediment that may have settled over the rocks or gravel.

Planting the aquarium completes the scene and must, therefore, be treated with careful attention. Sufficient swimming space must be allowed for fish.

The aquarium should be refilled by placing a sheet of newspaper over the lowered water surface and gently pouring water onto it. Having filled the tank to the required level, a thermometer is fixed and the filter and air-stone are connected. Finally, a 'cover-glass' is put over the top of the tank and the lighting hood is kept on it.

The aquarium is allowed to settle down for a period of 7-14 days, during which the plants will become established by producing new roots to anchor themselves into the gravel and, thereby, be less likely to be pulled loose by the fish. Very often the leaves of some of the plants will turn yellow and die, this is to be anticipated.

During the waiting period any chlorine and excess undissolved oxygen will be eliminated from the water, which will become safe for the well-begin of the fish. This process can be greatly assisted by running the filter or air-stone, thus causing a larger amount of the water to be exposed to the surface where the gaseous exchange takes place.

Control of light intensity, offering only sufficient food to be immediately eaten, regularly siphoning over the gravel, filtration and periodic partial water changes will ensure the best chances of the aquarium remaining in a healthy condition. Failure to remove decomposing debris will sooner or later result in pollution with consequential loss of fish.

Pond Fish Keeping

Types of Pond Keeping

The majority of garden ponds contain a range of coldwater fish species notably goldfish, carp, koi carp and tench and are often relatively well-planted. Accessories and equipment are usually kept to a minimum. However, the establishment of ponds especially for the maintenance of koi carp, usually with a minimum of submerged vegetation and sometimes with quite elaborate filtration systems, is increasing.

Important Considerations

Pond Construction

There are three basic methods of pond construction which include concrete, moulded glass fibre, and plastic or polythene flexible liners. The construction of a garden pond from concrete is hard work but permanent. Moulded pools are very easy to install but will be expensive and some are too shallow to maintain fish. Flexible liners are a popular choice 50 several types exist ranging from little more than a thin sheet of plastic or polythene to very tough butyl liners, which appear almost as permanent as a concrete of moulded pool.

Siting a Pond

A garden pond is best situated in an area of level ground where it receives some shade. It should not be sited below over-hanging trees and bushes (which may shed their leaves into the pool causing pollution), and the entry of fertilized or pesticide run-off into the pool should also be prevented. Naturally, a tap water supply will be needed to fill the pond.

Size of Ponds

A pond may be almost any size and shape although it should always have an area deeper than 1 m, to provide protection for the fish during the summer months. The garden ponds are always longer and wider than they are

Figure 16: Ornamental Fish Culture Ponds

deep and 2 m long, 1.5 m wide and 1 m deep is suggested as a minimum size. Very small ponds will be prone to overstocking and fluctuating water conditions. Netting material shall be used to cover the ponds for the entry of birds, snakes, frogs and other enemies.

Equipment

Small water pump fountain units add attractive water movement to the pond, as well as providing aeration in still weather. Such pumps can also be used to provide water for a waterfall and some can be converted to also carry out a small amount of mechanical and / or biological filtration.

Stocking Ponds

Plants

The plants can carry out a number of functions and their effect on algal growth and on stabilizing water conditions are pertinent in garden ponds.

The simplest and most convenient way to plant a pond is using the baskets. The baskets are best lined with clean sacking and then filled with unfertilized garden soil. Following careful planting of these baskets and before placing them into the pond, a layer of pebbles can be added to the basket to prevent fish disturbing the soil-causing discolouration of the water.

Fish

A smaller range of fish are generally kept in a garden pond and these fish are often limited to specifically ornamental varieties that are brightly coloured and easily visible. Some of the more unusual and long-finned varieties of goldfish are, however, a little delicate to be left in the pond throughout the year and may develop fin problems. Certain species of tropical freshwater fish can be kept in a garden pond during the warmer months.

Stocking Levels

Stocking should begin with a number of relatively inexpensive fish (to ensure there are no unforeseen problems) and then proceed towards the above-maximum figure over a few weeks. It is still unwise to stock a pond with too many fish too soon.

Quarantine

Since infectious diseases can be quite difficult to treat in a large garden pond, quarantine of all new fish is quite important. All new fish should be floated in their new home or in the quarantine tank for fifteen to twenty minutes, to let water temperatures equalize.

Chapter 6
Care of Goldfish

The goldfish is usually classified as a coldwater fish. Like most carp, goldfish produce a large amount of waste both in their faeces and through their gills, releasing harmful chemicals into the water. This also happens because goldfish, like other cyprinids, lack a stomach and only have an intestinal tract. Buildup of this waste to toxic levels can occur in a relatively short period of time, which is often the cause of a fish's sudden death. It may be the amount of water surface area, not the water volume, that decides how many goldfish may live in a container, because this determines how much oxygen diffuses and dissolves from the air into the water; one square foot of water surface area for every inch of goldfish length. If the water is being further aerated by way of water pump, filter or fountain, more goldfish may be kept in the container. The hardy breeds of goldfish are so rugged that few die from lack of attention.

Most goldfish that die before their time is because of three leading forms of overkindness.

The greatest cause of trouble is overfeeding. In wild, fish eat practically all the time that is because food is not too plentiful, and fish must scurry around the livelong day in an effort to find enough. By giving fish plenty to eat at the same time in an aquarium the fish will literally eat themselves to death. Another danger is crowding. Six or eight goldfish is an aquarium designed for three or four, or overcrowding, will soon separate the strong from the weak, and the weak will die. Too much sun and improper water temperatures, along with too frequent changing of the water, are also harmful.

Importance of Quality Water

Goldfish natively live in ponds, and other still or slow moving bodies of water in depths up to 20 m. Their native climate is subtropical to tropical and they live in freshwater with a pH of 6.0–8.0 and a temperature range of 4 to 41°C although they will not survive long at the higher temperatures. They are considered ill-suited even to live in a heated tropical fish tank, as they are used to the greater amount of oxygen in unheated tanks, and some believe that the heat burns them. However, goldfish have been observed living for centuries in outdoor ponds in which the temperature often raise about 30°C. Most aquarium pets are able to adjust quickly to the type of water it is easiest to provide for them.

The soft water is fine for fish. Highly chlorinated water should not be used. Deep well water may have too heavy mineral content. Swamp water, or any similar water which contains decomposing vegetation, is too acid. Natural, clear water dipped from a free-flowing steam or a pond in which fish and greenery live would be perfect water for the aquarium.

A filter system in the aquarium adds to the health of the fish, but is not necessary. In a filtering system the aquarium water is pumped by way of a tiny quiet motor through a chamber containing sand, activated charcoal, glass wool and other filtering materials. It changes the water in no way, except to keep it very clear.

An aerator helps, too. This is a simple hose extension from the pump and it releases a small and constant stream of air bubbles at the bottom of the aquarium. The aquarium water absorbs considerable oxygen from this air stream.

All aquarium fishes are sensitive to odors, especially the tropicals. Move them out of the rooms in which you plan to do any painting.

Feeding

Goldfish will eat practically anything. There are a number of excellent commercial feeds with a perfectly balanced content of food, salts, and minerals. What you feed goldfish is not nearly so important as how much you feed them. You cannot rear them properly if you feed them when they seem hungry, because they are always hungry, even hungry enough to beg. Indulge them occasionally, if you like, but infrequently and only with tidbits. Observe the fish as they eat what you throw to them. After a few days of watching, limit them to only as much food as they will consume in five minutes. Remove the surplus, for it becomes waterlogged, decomposes, fouls the water, and kills some of your fish.

Feed goldfish lightly and only once a day. If they become torpid and slow moving, try feeding them every other day, or every third day, and see if they don't become livelier. If they do, hold them to the lighter diet. By keeping fish hungry you keep them lively and comfortable, and prolong their lifespan by several years. It is far worse to overfeed than to underfeed, and the worst thing you can possible do is to load up your aquarium or pool with extra food when you go away for a weekend. It is better to let the goldfish miss a few meals. Do not feed them any heavier than usual when you return and resume the feeding schedule.

Food Variety

Goldfish thrive on variety in their diet from time to time. Feed them scraped or finely chopped oyster, clam, or shrimp–preferably raw–or earthworms, if you want to go to the trouble of digging and chopping them. The larger fish–3 to 4 inches or longer–seem to consider freshly swatted flies a delicacy. Any of these things, however, are to be given instead of the regular food, not in addition to it.

Space to Live

Goldfish hovering near the surface of the water, "blowing bubbles", "playing", or "just being friendly", are a pretty sight to anyone who knows nothing about them. However, all indicate a cruel situation, for they are sure signs of suffocation.

Plenty of room for living is vitally important to goldfish, for living room is also "breathing" room. As fish breath water and extract oxygen from it, the water absorbs more oxygen from the air. This absorption is not rapid, and considerable water surface must be exposed to provide enough absorption to sustain life properly. To illustrate, a 6 cm goldfish needs all the oxygen that can be absorbed in about 50 square inches of water surface; that means the entire water surface of a 7- by 6.5 cm square bowl or of a circular bowl 8 inches in diameter at the water level.

Rules of Capacity

Figure out the water-surface area in square inches. For square or oblong pools and aquariums, multiply width by length. In round bowls and pools, multiply pi (3.1426 or 22/7ths) by the square of the radius. Simply estimate the surface area of irregular pools and, to be on the safe side, make your estimate low.

With the area of the water surface determined, stock the pool or aquarium with no more than 1 inch of fish (not counting the tail) for every 20 square inches of water surface. As an example, a 10- by 12-inch aquarium would present 120 square inches of water surface. That would allow comfortably for 6 inches of fish–one 6-inch fish, six 1-inch fish, three 2-inch fish, or any other length combinations you want. Allow the more elaborate forms–Veiltails, Moors, and so on–25 square inches of water surface to every inch of fish.

Then consider that the larger the fish, the more oxygen it requires per inch of length. A 5- or 6-inch goldfish, for example, uses more oxygen than five or six 1-inch fish. This does not amount to a very great increase in oxygen needed, but in an aquarium full of fish it is an appreciable factor. So, once again, play safe by keeping your estimate low and tend to under stock rather than overstock.

Temperature

Goldfish do their best in water temperatures of 26–32°C. Whatever the temperature in which fish live, it is important to keep it constant, with no sudden changes.

In Aquariums

The water temperature in an aquarium requires more consideration, but it is easy to maintain at a safe point, too. Goldfish do well in winter in a room comfortable for human beings. Except for unheated corners of the basement, extremely cold bed rooms, and southern windows which get sun all day. Almost any place in the house will do for an aquarium, as long as it has about two hours of direct sunlight daily.

Amount of Sun

Ideally, an aquarium should be placed where there is two hours of direct sunlight daily. This much light playing upon the oxygenating plants will enable them to do their good work efficiently, and yet it is not enough to make the water dangerously warm.

Sunlight is harmful if it causes too much plant action in the aquarium, resulting in an overabundance of algae and other microscopic green growth. Check excess growth, try covering the sunny side of the aquarium with coloured cellophane or with coloured or white paper.

Avoiding Shock

An sudden cause of death among goldfish is shock, the effect of which is often not noticeable right away.

They suffer shock most often while being transferred from the pet store to their new home, or while the pool or aquarium water is being changed. The shock in the first instance is slight and necessary; in the second instance, it is unnecessary and can be fatal. When you clean an aquarium, don't draw a bucket or huge jar of cold water from the tap, gather the goldfish in a net, dump them into it, and leave them there for two or three hours while you scrub and refill the aquarium, and then dump the fish back into fresh, clean, cold water. This is shocking treatment because it is completely different from anything fish might encounter under natural conditions. For fish, there is no such thing as a sudden natural change. Fish subjected to such shock probably won't show the ill effects immediately. A day or two afterwards, however, a dozen different goldfish may display a dozen different ailments, all results of shock-sluggishness, congested fins and tails, a dull, filmy covering on the scales, and so on. Most of them will probably recover in time, particularly if doctored. Such continues shocks, however, will keep them in poor condition, and drastically reduce their normal lifespan.

How to Change Aquarium Water

Changing aquarium water can be a simple. The easiest procedure is to transfer the fish in the old water into another container. Then clean the aquarium, refill it, and let it stand for two or three hours before you move the fish back into it. This allows the fresh water to approach proper temperature and also permits the release of any unnatural gases–an important consideration if you live in a community where water is heavily chlorinated.

Aquarium Maintenance

Scrub your aquarium with practically any preparation that cuts dirt will for you in other household jobs, and rinse it thoroughly before putting it back into service. Accumulated dirt and algae on the sides are best removed by scraping with a razor blade, then scrubbing with soap or detergent and water, with or without ammonia added.

Plastic or copper sponge is used on the stubborn spots. Aquarium should not be scoured with sand or other abrasive, as this in time will dull the glass with hundreds of minute scratches.

Green Water

Whatever, kind of an aquarium you have and wherever you place it, the water will eventually take on a greenish colour, because of the growth of millions of tiny aquatic plants, mostly algae.

Too much algae become unsightly before they are dangerous to fish. When the aquarium water becomes practically opaque, try to find the cause.

An over crowded aquarium is often the answer. Double-check the number and size of fish you have, and make sure your capacity calculations were correct. If overcrowding is the cause, the situation will right itself soon after a few fish have been removed.

Too much sunlight is another cause. Remember that the aquarium should get direct sun for only two hours a day. If it is getting more than, two hours, and algae are too numerous, try cutting down the strength of the light by pasting white or coloured tissue paper over the sunny side of the aquarium.

Dying Algae

Heavy growth of algae in aquarium should be avoided because the water will often undergo a chemical change which will kill off the whole algae mass. Once they begin to die, the water will become brownish yellow. The water should be changed immediately or else decomposing algae generate gases that kill goldfish.

Cloudy Water

Cloudy water in an aquarium, unless it is extremely overcrowded, is caused by only one process–decomposition. There may be a dead fish or snail, or accumulated bits of food. There is only one way to correct it and that is to change the water.

Chapter 7
Foods and Feeding

The goldfish is omnivorous, and there is little in the way of food that will not be eaten. Live foods, fresh, frozen or dried animal and vegetable matter will be readily accepted. Indeed, the diet should be as varied as possible. Goldfish have lived for years on a diet of commercially prepared dried foods, but their growth and development does not compare with a fish that has had its diet supplemented with live foods of one sort or another. Goldfish are opportunistic feeders. When an excess of food is offered, they will produce more waste and faeces, partly due to incomplete digestion. Overfed fish can sometimes be recognized by faeces trailing from their cloaca. Goldfish need only be fed as much food as they can consume in one to two minutes, and no more than twice a day. Extreme overfeeding can be fatal, typically by bursting of the intestines. This happens most often with selectively bred goldfish, which have a convoluted intestinal tract as opposed to a straight one in common goldfish. Special goldfish food has a lower protein and higher carbohydrate content. It is sold in two consistencies–flakes that float at the top of the aquarium, and pellets that sink slowly to the bottom.

The goldfish requires protein, fat, carbohydrates, minerals and vitamins in its food, combined in the correct proportions to grow strong and healthy.

Proteins

Proteins are composed of amino acids, and are the compounds from which the essential tissues are formed. Approximately twenty-one amino acids have been isolated, although not all may be necessary to life, however, those which are termed 'essential amino acids'. In the digestive system of the goldfish protein is broken down into amino acids to aid its growth. A good food should contain at least 25 per cent protein.

Fats

Fats are another source of energy. In the intestine the fats are converted into fatty acids and glycerides, in which form they are absorbed into the body, any excess being stored by the body as tissues. These fatty tissues are also made up of carbohydrates and protein. The tissues serve as a store for the fat-soluble vitamins A, D, E and K. An excess of fat-producing foods can seriously harm the goldfish, by causing malfunction of the kidneys, and give rise to fatty degeneration of the liver. Foods containing an excessive amount of fat should be avoided –4 per cent is about the right amount.

Carbohydrates

These are the starches and sugars found in the food, and serves as a source of energy, while aiding the utilization of fats. Many of the plants upon which the goldfish browse consist largely of carbohydrates, and have a nutritive value. In the intestine the carbohydrates are converted into simple sugars, and may be absorbed or stored in the liver and other organs. Too much sugar can cause the liver to become enlarged, and this may result in the death of the fish. The minimum carbohydrate content of a good food should not be less than 45 per cent.

Vitamins

Vitamins are just as essential to the goldfish as they are to humans: without them they will suffer from vitamin deficiency. The vitamin requirements will be found in fresh uncooked vegetable matter; however, prepared food must be vitamin enriched. A good food will contain vitamins A, D, E, K, B_1, B_2, B_6 and C. One in particular, carotene or pro-vitamin A, is necessary to the good colouring of the goldfish. It is found in salt-water algae, dark green freshwater algae, egg yolk, and the shell of the shrimp. Carrots also contain carotene.

Minerals

Minerals, such as cobalt, iodine, copper, iron, manganese and zinc, are also essential for the well-being of the goldfish. Some, though necessary, are only required in minute quantities, but, if missing the organic balance of the fish will be upset. The best commercially prepared foods will contain minerals in the correct amount. A varied diet, including live foods, will ensure that the fish receives an adequate supply of the necessary minerals.

Foods

Foods may be commercially prepared dried foods, home-made foods, frozen foods, various live foods and foods from the household.

Figure 17: Artificial Feed

Live Foods

Live foods like tubifex, daphnia, moina and artemia are regarded by most aquarists as the best form of food, because they are the natural foods that would be eaten in the wild. There is no doubt that fish which are allowed a regular feed of live food, as part of their diet, appear to be more lively than those fed solely upon dried foods.

Earthworm

Earthworm is well recognized as one of the best live foods for bringing goldfish into breeding condition. Easily

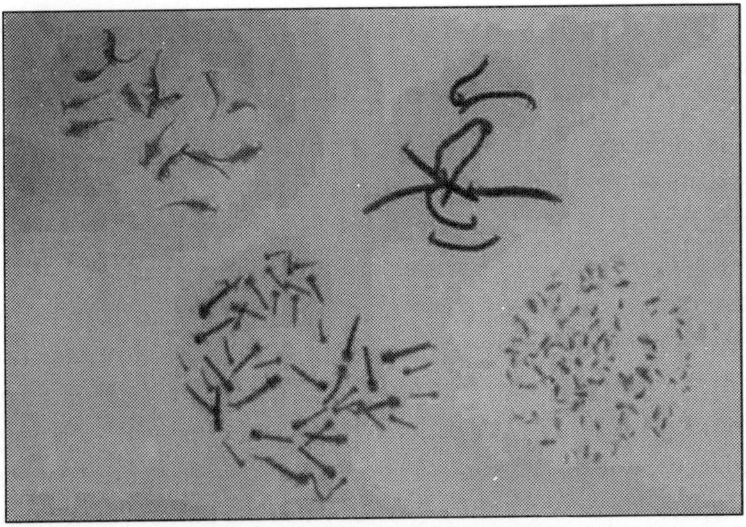

Figure 18: Live Food Organisms

obtained during most seasons of the year, it is readily accepted and acts as a mild laxative.

The red and pink worms, up to about two inches (51 mm) long are best; larger worms tend to be tough and not so easily digested. The collected worms should first be swilled to remove any soil or slimy mud which may adhere to them. The very small worms can be fed straight to the fish; however, those more than half-an-inch (13 mm) long should be chopped into suitable lengths. It is not necessary to give a further wash, this would only swill away the digested vegetable matter which forms part of this excellent food. It will be seen that the fish will spit out any unwanted matter.

White Worms

White worm is an easily cultivated one and grows to around three-quarters of an inch. Most pet fish stores can usually supply a starter culture. It is a very popular food amongst goldfish enthusiasts because of its ready availability, ease of cultivation, and acceptability by the fish.

A lidless wooden box, of about twelve inches (305 mm) square and six inches (152 mm) deep was made and half filled with mixture of sterilized loam and peat. The peat should be thoroughly soaked and then squeezed, to remove the excess water. Make a fifty/fifty mixture of the loam and peat and lightly firm into the box. Take care that no ants or other life are introduced. A shallow hollow is then made in the soil and filled with food, the worms being placed on top. The soil is covered with a loose fitting piece of glass to conserve the moisture, and the box covered with a board to exclude the light. The food for the worms may consist of soaked bread, saltless mashed potatoes. The box is placed in an airy place, with a temperature of about 22°C. The food supply is replenished as it is consumed, or after removing any uneaten spoilt food, until the worms have established a thriving colony. It will be found that they will gather in thick clusters around the food, and it is a simple matter to roll them into a ball to be picked up and fed to the fish. It usually takes around a month before the worms have increased sufficiently to start feeding them to the fish.

Micro Worms

Micro worms are an ideal food for small goldfish because of their small size–less than 1/8 inch (3 mm). To avoid any unpleasant smell, and to keep the worms thriving, a new culture should be started every five to six days. Shallow plastic dishes make good containers and these should have a little pre-cooked cereal, made into a stiff paste, spread thinly over the bottom of the dish. The starter culture is added by smearing over the surface of the cooled food. It is covered with a sheet of glass and keep at room temperature. After a few days the surface of the culture will be found to be seething with the tiny worms. If a knife-blade is scraped around the inner edge of the dish the worms will be collected; clean and ready to swill into the fish tank. After about five days the culture will start to 'go off'. Fresh cultures will need to be started, preferably arranging a slight overlap in time between each culture.

Daphnia, Moina

Daphnia, the well known water Flea, and an attractive food to goldfish. It should be remembered that daphnia breathe through gills and deprive fish of essential oxygen, so do not feed too many at a time. Daphnia have a transparent chitinous carapace, and vary in size according to age and genera–up to 1/5 inch (5 mm). The colour can also vary being red, green or almost black, depending upon their food source. Food may be algae, bacteria or infusoria. The bright red colour of some daphnia is due to haemoglobin, as the oxygen content of the water becomes lower so the haemoglobin increases and there by causes the blood to become a deeper red.

Daphnia can be found in many aquatic habitats, but mainly where heavy decomposition is taking place. Stagnant pools, ponds and farm-yard pools are some of the likely places in which daphnia may be found. To collect this food a fine-mesh net should be used.

Cyclops

Another small crustacean so named because of its single eye. They feed upon similar foods to the daphnia and are generally most abundant during the warmer months of the year. Cyclops are found in the same waters as daphnia and will often be found as part of the daphnia haul. They are good food, especially for the smaller fish.

Tubifex

Considered by many aquarists to be one of the finest live foods for goldfish. It is a thread-like worm, slightly over an inch (25 mm) in length, and reddish in colour. They live, often in large colonies, in areas of high pollution and organic decomposition, where they bury their heads in the mud and ooze. The larger part of the body waves in an undulating motion in the water to breathe in the dissolved oxygen–if disturbed the tails are withdrawn into the black silt at lightning speed. Areas near the outfalls of raw sewage are often densely colonized by these tubificids, where they appear as a red mass of waving tails.

Collecting tubifex from such sites is a filthy and smelly business, and the collector should dress accordingly. A strong, fine-meshed net should be thrust quickly into the ooze and withdrawn. If the mud is then tipped into a sieve made of 2 inch-high (51 mm) frame and a bottom pierced by 1/8 inch (3 mm) holes, the muck can be swilled. This will separate much of the filth from the worms. The balls of worms can then be carried home in plastic bags for further cleaning.

To clean the worms, they are placed into shallow containers into which a continuous flow of water is run. The period of cleaning should last for around three days, until the internal matter has been flushed out of the tubifex. Only when the worms are thoroughly cleaned they should be offered to the fish.

Bloodworms

The larvae of the Chironomidae–the midge fly–easily recognized by its blood-red colour and figure-of-eight swimming motion. The larva, which is not a worm, grows to around 1/2 inch (13 mm) in length and is available throughout the year. Highly satisfactory food for the goldfish, it can be found in almost all fresh waters, but they are usually found to be most abundant in or on the bottom debris of lakes, ponds, pools and slow moving streams, and even rainwater barrels.

Mosquito Larvae

Mosquito larvae is referred to as wrigglers. Almost black in colour, they are up to 1/4 inch (16 mm) long and hang head down from the water surface. When disturbed they leave the surface with a whipping movement but, due to their dependence upon atmospheric air, will quickly return. They feed upon microscopic food. Mosquito larvae will be found in most still waters.

The female mosquito lays her eggs in black canoe-shaped rafts during warm summer evenings. These may be collected and floated on the water surface of aquariums containing fry; as the eggs hatch the fry will eat the tiny larvae. The larger larvae are best caught with a daphnia net. Normally no cleaning is necessary before being given to the fish. However, not to feed too many at once because any that are not eaten can turn into adult mosquitoes.

Chapter 8
Breeding

Goldfish breed when they are a year old, and sometimes at the age of nine months. They continue to breed up to the age of six or seven, and there is a record of Fantails breeding at the age of ten. The best breeding age is between three and four. If old fish are chosen four males should be placed with three females; if young fish, then, four males with six females. It is best for the fish to be all about the same size, but if the females are much bigger than the males then six males should be placed with three females. The female fish should be at least 2 inch long.

The body of the berried female becomes swollen, denoting the presence of ova. At the same time the male develops tubercles, each about the size of a pin's head, denoting the presence of testes. The tubercles (sometimes called 'pearl organs') are usually confined to the gill-covers, but they may extend to the skin of the back, and to the pectoral fins. They disappear as soon as spawning has been completed, and it would seem that in some males they never develop.

Sl.No.	Male	Female
1.	Flat belly	Swollen belly
2.	Tubercles otherwise called pearl organs present on the pectoral fin [this is white pin head in size]	No symptom
3.	While pressing milt oozes out	Egg oozes out
4.	Vent whitish	Vent pinkish

The selected fish should be carefully conditioned. This is most important. Constipation must be avoided, and dried foods should not be given in any large quantity. The earthworms are best food for bringing than into good breeding condition, and these should be the staple diet. They

Figure 19: Watering in the Cement Cistern

Figure 20: Introducing Aquatic Weed

may be varied with *Daphnia,* bloodworms and *Tubifex.* During the conditioning period the water should be kept at a temperature of about 25ºC. This has been found to be the best feeding temperature. The fish should be kept under these conditions until the male fish begin to show interest in the females. They are then transferred to the spawning pond, the temperature of which should be slightly higher than 25ºC. The hardier breeds of goldfish spawn best at temperatures between 25ºC and 30ºC and the increase in temperature helps the spawning act. Rain, or watering the pond, is said to encourage the fish.

Since goldfish eggs are adhesive. Natural or artificial substratum should be used for the attachment of eggs. The natural substratum is aquatic plants like *Hydrilla, Ceratophyllum* and *Myriophyllum* can be used. Before introducing these plants in to the breeding tank, these are

Figure 21: Introducing the Fishes

Figure 22: . Feeding the Fishes

to be immersed in 2 ppm potassium permanganate solution to remove all pathogens attached to the plant. Nylon fibrils are usually used as artificial substratum. The weight of the substratum should be 5 or 6 times more than that of breeders. Chinese breeders use large quantities of *Ceratophyllum*, so much so that in China it is popularly known as goldfish weed.

Soon the males begin to chase the females. After a day or two of aimless chasing, the spawning-drive begins in earnest. The drive consists of the males pursuing the females to and fro across the aquarium or pond. The drive, which continues for about two or three hours, until the female is stripped of eggs, is an attempt on the part of the male to bump the abdomen of the female and so facilitate the release of the ova. Finally, the female sinks to the bottom of the aquarium or pond. By means of his snout the male lifts the female until she is on top of the plants and almost out of the water. It is now that the eggs are released. They are released in batches (the first batch is best: the last is likely to produce weak fry) and each batch is immediately fertilized by the male. A female goldfish in good condition releases a large number of eggs at one spawning. The number of eggs depends very much on the size of the fish, but in general a medium-sized female goldfish of size 50g releases anything up to 3,000 eggs. These figures, however, apply only to a first spawning, and fewer eggs are released subsequently.

Spawning usually takes place between four o'clock and nine o'clock in the morning, but sometimes late in the afternoon. Whenever, it is thought that the fish have spawned, the bunches of aquatic plants should be carefully examined for eggs. If eggs are seen adhering to the plants, the plants should be transferred to a bucket, which has been half-filled with water from the spawning pond, and taken indoors.

The eggs should not be removed from the aquatic plants, but the plants with the eggs adhering to them should be distributed among the aquaria, allowing from ten to twenty eggs to every 4 litres of water. When the eggs are transferred, care must be taken to ensure that the water is from the spawning pond. Fertile eggs are of a yellowish colour, becoming paler and more difficult to see on the second and third days after release. Infertile eggs, attacked by fungus, turn white opaque and fuzzy, and sink to the bottom of the aquarium. They should be removed at once with a pipette, or their presence will assist the spread of the disease, particularly if the temperature of the water is low.

The period of incubation depends upon the temperature of the water and the condition of the eggs. Japanese breeders incubate the eggs in water at a temperature of 15 to 20°C, and at this heat the eggs hatch in about eight or nine days. It is advisable to incubate the eggs in water at a temperature of 25 to 30 degrees, when the eggs hatch in 2 to 3 days. By raising or lowering the temperature, it is possible to hasten or retard the period of incubation, but it is not desirable to do so.

The development of the embryo within the egg depends on the period of incubation, which, as we have seen, in turn depends on the temperature of the water. In an incubation period of three days, the embryo can be distinguished on the first day as an elongated tube, tapering to the posterior extremity, and coiled around the large yolk-sac. On the second day the head is enlarged, and the eyes as yet unpigmented can be distinguished. The yolk-sac is much diminished in size, and free at the posterior extremity of the embryo. On the third day the eyes are pigmented with black, and the pupils can clearly be seen as circular areas in the centers. Pigment spots can be discerned on the body. The yolk-sac is attached only to the lower surface of the head and the anterior third of the body. The beating of the heart and the flow of the blood can be observed. The contractions of the embryo are more frequent and more vigorous than formerly, as the pulsations of the heart increase with age (and temperature). As the embryo develops, its contractions become more and more restless, until it bursts the egg-membrane in the region of its back; soon its tail is freed; it makes an effort to swim and quickly free its head.

On emergence from the egg, the larva is about one-fifth of an inch long. In general shape it resembles a tadpole. The dorsal region is greenish in colour, with scattered irregular pigment spots. The rest of the body is translucent. At this stage the larvae hang at rest (occasionally) labouring for short distances, some to the aquatic plants, others to the sides of the aquarium, still others at the surface of the water. On no account they should be disturbed. No food need be given to them. At this stage they exist by absorbing the remains of the yolk. Meanwhile the liver develops, and from the upper part of the oesophagus a little out-growth becomes a glistening silvery sac–the well-known air-bladder.

About forty-eight hours after hatching, the yolk has been entirely absorbed and the larva is now known as a post-larva. It is free-swimming; for it is provided with a pair of pectoral fins, and a median fin running along the back, round the tail, and along the underside to the vent. Later the median fin breaks up to form the dorsal, caudal and anal fins. The pelvic fins develop much later.

The little fish now begins to swim in search of the microscopic organisms that are present in all mature water and on which they feed. But in an aquarium this natural food will not last for long and artificial feeding must be given.

It is at this point that most aquarist fail. The high rate of mortality among newly-hatched goldfish is mainly due to the fact that most inexperienced aquarists rarely supply them with sufficient infusoria during the first two or three weeks after hatching. A plentiful and continuous supply of microscopic forms of life is the great secret of raising a fair quantity of strong healthy fish, and it is wonderful how much their future growth and strength depends on the amount of correct live food (or suitable substitutes) supplied during the first few weeks'.

Another artificial food for fry is the yolk of a hard-boiled egg rubbed between the fingers so that it is distributed in the water as a fine cloud. It is best to feed goldfish-fry on infusoria. It has been shown that fry fed on dried foods do not grow nearly so rapidly as those fed on live foods.

Water containing infusoria should not smell. It should look as though a grayish-white dust is suspended in it. The culture must be kept fresh, and the best way to do this is to aerate the water in which the infusoria are living.

The appetites of goldfish-fry vary so much that it is impossible to say how much food should be given to them.

A general rule with some breeders is to feed the fry five times a day for the first three weeks or so, then three times a day for a few more weeks, then twice daily, finally, at the end of three months, once a day.

At the age of about four weeks the fry are ready to take bigger food than infusoria. Very small *Daphnia* and *Cyclops* are the usual foods, and they may be given by placing a quantity in a muslin bag and suspending it in the water. The bag should be left in the water for about half an hour at a time. During this period the smallest of the *Daphnia* and *Cyclops* will escape into the aquarium.

Infusoria

In the old days, before the advent of Brine Shrimp eggs, this was the live food most commonly cultured-some goldfish breeders still use it. Infusoria was a collective name given to microscopic unicellular organisms. There are many ways of cultivating infusoria, some giving better results than others. Six or so large glass jars are filled with water from an established pond or aquarium. The water is strained through some very fine material to exclude any small insects or other creatures. Into these jars the following vegetable matter is added; chopped dry hay, dried leaves of aquatic plants, rotten cabbage leaves, rotten potatoes, bruised banana skins, and so forth. The jars are then placed in a warm dark place for a period of about five days. At the end of this period a good culture of microscopic food should be visible. Water containing infusoria almost always has a bad smell and looks as though a grayish-white cloud of dust is suspended in it. The culture must be kept fresh by gentle aeration. It must also be fed, and this is best done by adding a small amount of decomposing cabbage leaf from time-to-time. Fresh cultures are set up exactly as before, having a small amount of an existing culture added to speed up the cultivation.

The method of feeding to the goldfish fry is quite simple. A jar of infusoria is stood slightly above the tank, and a short length of air-line tubing is used to siphon the water from the jar into the fry-tank. Normally an air-line clip is used to regulate the flow to a slow drip. Thus the food could be left to 'drip-feed' the fry continuously, the supply jar being topped-up from the other cultures as needed. Every effort must be made to see that the temperature of the infusoria water is near to that of the tank water, otherwise the infusoria could be killed, and so pollute the water in which the fry were swimming.

Chapter 9

Health Care

As in any health program, prevention is far more effective than remedial treatment. Here are a few measures, which may keep the health of the aquarium at the highest possible level.

To Keep Goldfish Healthy

1. Over stocking to be strictly avoided.
2. Sterilize new aquatic plants before introducing in the Aquarium.
3. Sterilize new goldfish for an hour or two in a potassium permanganate solution before adding in the Aquarium.
4. Watch for drooping dorsal fins (on fish which normally hold them stiff), for sluggishness, congested fins, and excrement containing slime or bubbles.

5. The ailing fish needs to be isolated immediately and treated according to symptoms.
6. Sterilize dipnets and containers used for treating fish with the potassium permanganate solution.

Quarantine Tank

Diseased fish removed for treatment should be kept in a broad, shallow tray in only 2.5 to 7 cm of water. A dish pan, can be used as quarantine tank washtub or partially filled goldfish bowl. The water in the treatment receptacle should be of the same temperature, as that in which the fish have been living. Keep the ailing fish out of strong light, and suspend feeding, while they are being treated.

Green Water Treatment

Any tired, sluggish fish seem to revive immediately upon transfer to different water. This water, if green, is all the more beneficial. A good provision to make for treatment is a spare aquarium planted with a few oxygenating plants and kept ready for use.

Mud-bottom Treatment

For the lesser ills, as a run-down condition, transfer the fish for a few days to shallow temporary quarters, such as an old washtub, with 5 to 7 cm of mud in the bottom.

Salt Treatment

Sea water, 1 part to 5 parts of fresh water, makes the best salt solution. If this is unavailable, use rock salt, 2 heaping teaspoons to 4 litres of water. Table salt can be used, in the same proportion, but use a pure brand that has no inert matter added to prevent caking. Change the salt water daily during the treatment. A common procedure is to increase the strength of the solution daily, over a period of three to four days, until it is twice a strong as it was originally. After two days, or when the fish show improvement, begin weakening the solution and taper it down gradually to the original strength before returning the fish to pool or aquarium. Remove fish from the solution immediately if they show signs of exhaustion by rolling over.

Potassium Permanganate Treatment

For treating the whole ponds of goldfish with potassium permanganate, add 1.5g potassium permanganate to 400 litres of water. For a smaller volume of water, allow approximately 1–4 litres. This is on the strong side, but when we treat huge ponds of fish, we take into consideration the great amount of algae and other plant growth on which the chemical will expend part of its strength.

From 1/8 to 1/4 grain per 4 litres is a good solution strength for treatment of fish in smaller containers. Leave them in the solution for two days, or until they show signs of exhaustion.

Potassium permanganate can be directly added into pond or aquarium, it will act as a tonic to aquatic plants and other goldfish there. But the snails, needs to be removed or else for the solution may kill them. Potassium permanganate will also kill off most of the algae in the pond or aquarium.

Some ailments require repeated treatments with potassium permanganate, but such treatments should not be given more often than every ten days. The water need not be changed between treatments, for the chemical expends its energy in two to three days, and the strength is not cumulative.

Ammonia Treatment

The effects of an ammonia solution–10 drops of household ammonia to 4 litres of water–are sometimes beneficial. Leave the ailing fish, in the solution for 5 minutes, or until there are signs of distress.

Constipation

The excrement of a healthy fish is brown, usually in long sections, and without bubbles or slime. Any change in this particularly if coupled with sluggish behaviour, indicates constipation. There are several easy cures. Sprinkling a pinch of Epsom salts into the water every week as prevention, or giving scrambled eggs, chopped lettuce leaves, spinach, or chopped earth-worms as laxative foods.

Since overfeeding is a common cause of constipation, reduce the diet a bit after recovery.

Dropsy

This ailment, which seems to be confined mostly to tropical and fancier breeds, is one of the worst, but comparatively rare. The affected fish seem well except that the body swells and the scales stand out at an angle, like the seeds of a pine cone. Fish may live several days with dropsy, but there is no known cure for it.

Fin Congestion

This is a common ill, especially among fancier breeds, blood circulation is poor in filmy fin and tail surfaces, rendering them highly susceptible to ailment. Fins and tails become bloodshot, and in extreme cases split and fray.

This usually develops from overfeeding, cold water, sudden chill or other shock, or overcrowding.

The salt-water treatment for a couple of days is best. Two days in the potassium permanganate solution is also good. Feeding should be stopped for the ailing fish during treatment, and the diet should be reduced somewhat after recovery.

Gill Congestion

This seems to be an advanced stage of gill fever which tends to attack fish about a year old and approximately 2 inches long. Gills swell, and the infection covers the throat with a grayish-white discolouration.

Fish should be treated into a strong salt solution–6 or 7 teaspoons to 4 litres–and leave it there until it collapses.

Gill Fever

It is prevalent among small fry up to five or six weeks old. Gills swell and become inflamed, and the fever kills within a few days. It is so contagious.

Swimming Bladder Trouble

Fish affected with swimming bladder trouble rest on the bottom of pool or aquarium, or hand upside-down, or at an angle near the surface, and move only with apparent effort. When the bladder is affected, they lose all sense of balance. Scaleless fish and fish with shortened bodies are the most susceptible.

These symptoms may also be caused by stomach gases formed by indigestion. Any fish with such symptoms should be treated for constipation. If that treatment does not cure, it is best to destroy the fish.

Tail Congestion

The most common cause of this ailment is the shock experienced by fish during transportation. The base of the tail becomes densely bloodshot, and the congestion moves forward to other areas of the body. It is fatal unless checked. The salt-water treatment can cure this problems.

Tail Rot

This manifests itself in a splitting and ragged disintegration beginning at the end of tail and fins and moving towards the body. If it reaches the body it will be fatal.

Tail rot is quickly cured by the salt-water treatment. If the fins and tail of the recovered fish are unsightly, hold the fish down on a wet board and trim them with a sharp knife. Swab the trimmed edges with a potassium permanganate solution.

Tuberculosis

This is serious and difficult to cure. It is better to destroy them. When affected, a fish stops moving around, stops eating, and wastes away until the body has shrunken far out of proportion to the head.

Eye Inflammation

Gold fish with telescopic eyes are more prone than others to injuries about the eye, and these injuries sometimes cause the whole eye to become inflamed.

The inflammation can be swabed with boric-acid solution. Or use 1 part iodine and 9 parts glycerine. Usually a single application of either solution is sufficient.

Cuts, abrasions, and infections on goldfish are best treated by swabbing with kerosene, with the iodine-glycerine mixture, or with household mercurochrome.

The salt-water treatment alone usually helps a goldfish recover quickly from bruises.

Lost Scales

A goldfish which loses scales in a fight or an accident will grow new ones in time, unless other injuries are too severe. The salt-water treatment for a day or so will give it a good start toward recovery.

Parasites

Anchor Worm (*Lernea*)

This threadlike parasite is about half an inch long, and attaches itself with a firm grip on the bodies of goldfish. It is more annoying than dangerous to fish.

The whole aquarium or pool should be treated with potassium permanganate, 1/8 grain per gallon in the aquarium, 1/4 grain per gallon in the pool. It is necessary to repeat the treatment three times at ten-day intervals. The worm itself must be pulled from the goldfish for immediate relief. The head or anchor, if not removed from the fish by hand, will drop off in time.

Flukes

Flukes are microscopic parasite worms which attach themselves to the gills, causing the fish to breathe rapidly and to come to the surface frequently for gulps of air. The affected fishes will not take feed and die of starvation and exhaustion.

If the fish are in an aquarium, treat all of them. Disinfect the aquarium and refill it with clean water. If they are in an outdoor pool, examine all the fish and take out the affected ones for treatment.

A solution of 5 drops of formaldehyde to 1 quart of water is prepared and the affected fishes are immersed in the solution for 10 minutes. This treatment is repeated twice.

Ich (White Spot Disease)

A fish that spends an appreciable amount of time rubbing against plant stems and other solid objects, or "scratching" himself along the sandy bottom of the aquarium, probably has an itch caused by one of several forms of parasites.

This white parasite is less than half an large as the head of a pin, but when several hundred attach themselves to a goldfish it seems to be covered by a grayish white mantle.

There are several treatments. For every 4 litres of water in the aquarium, 1 drop of household Mercurochrome is added. After a cure is achieved, usually in about a week, change the aquarium water. Before returning the fish to the aquarium, swab the affected parts with Mercurochrome, full strength, or with kerosene.

Aquariums should be cleaned and disinfected after a cure, to get rid of the eggs of the parasite that may settle to the bottom, hatch, and begin the process all over again.

The potassium permanganate treatment is also effective, and this is the only practical treatment for outdoor pools in which Ichthyophthirius has been discovered.

Leeches

These are more of an annoyance than a danger to larger fish, but leeches can kill small fry. The white aquatic leech, about 1/2 inch long and lender, attaches itself to the bodies and gills of goldfish.

All affected fish are given progressive salt-water treatment. The aquarium is scrubed disinfected it with a solution of 1 teaspoon of ammonia for every 25 litres of water, and aquatic plants are disinfected in the same solution.

Lice

Fish lice are flat, transparent, and about the size of a pinhead. If enough attach themselves to the body they can be fatal. Fish with lice will rub vigorously against any solid object they can find. The parasite's blood-sucking, much like that of a mosquito's, creates a red spot on the fish.

The whole aquarium or the whole pool is treated with potassium permanganate when lice are detected.

White Fungus

This is a parasitic fungus present in almost all aquarium or pool water, but one which healthy fish easily resist. A run-down fish overcome by the fungus is marked by a white scum which appears first on tail and fins, and then spreads to the body. When it enters the gills, it kills the fish. Often goldfish die before the fungus gets to the gills.

White fungus is very contagious. All affected fish are removed immediately and subject them to the salt-water treatment.

Chapter 10

Marketing and Economics

The growing popularity of ornamental fish keeping is reflected in ubiquitous aquaria that features as an integral part of modern interior decoration. The aquarium fishes are thus gaining importance not only because of their aesthetic value but also due to their immense commercial value in the export trade world over. There has been considerable growth and diversification in the International trade of ornamental fishes, which is to the tune of about US$ 5 billion. The major traders include USA, Europe, Japan, Australia, Singapore, Indonesia and Philippines. India's share in ornamental fish trade is estimated to be around 5 crore rupees. However, it may be possible for India to capture at least 10 per cent of the present market utilizing its vast indigenous stock of germplasm and unemployed manpower.

Ornamental Fish Trade

The FAO statistics indicated that the world export of ornamental fish steadily rose from US$ 160.7 million since 1999 to a peak of US$ 282.6 million in 2006. Most of the world's supplies of ornamental fishes are from Asian countries. Singapore is the largest exporter of ornamental fish contributing 21.70 per cent followed by Spain, Czech Republic and Malaysia during 2006 (Dey, 2008). USA is the world's largest single market for ornamental fishes and imported US$ 48.40 million worth of fish in 2006, followed by UK (US$ 30.80 million) and Japan (US$ 27.20 million).

The ornamental fish market can be divided into four main sectors. The largest sector is the tropical freshwater species sector, which occupies about 80–90 per cent of the market. The other sectors are tropical marine and brackish water species, including invertebrates; coldwater (freshwater) species, mainly goldfish and koi and cold water marine and brackish water species.

In all there are about 1600 species of ornamental fish in the market, out of which 750 are freshwater species. More and more species are being added to the list as a result of advances in breeding, transport and aquarium technology. Some 90 per cent of the species are cultured while the remaining 10 per cent are collected from the wild. The annual world turnover for ornamental fish aquaculture is estimated at about US$ 200 million. The marine fish species constitute about 20 per cent of the market. About 95 per cent of marine fish are collected from the wild while 5 per cent are bred fish.

The price of an ornamental fish is considerably higher than the price of a fish destined for human consumption.

On average, there is a ratio of 1:100 between prices of food fish and aquarium fish. In general, marine ornamental fish have higher unit value compared to freshwater ornamental fish. The freshwater species dominating the market are mainly from the families *Poecilidae, Characidae, Cyprinidae,* and *Cichlidae.* The main species are guppy, platy, swordtail, molly, goldfish neon tetra, angelfish, zebra danio and discus. The guppy and the neon tetra represent more than 25 per cent of the world market in volume and more than 14 per cent in value.

The Supply Situation

World exports of ornamental fish rose from US$ 125.819 million in 1996. There was a dip during 1997–98 to a low of US$ 162.399 million in 1998 after which exports rose again to US$ 182.668 million in 2001. The downtrend during 1996-98 is attributed mainly to the Asian financial crisis.

With a share of 22.8 per cent (US$ 41.58 million), Singapore was the world's largest exporter in 2001. It is also the main trading hub for Asia. Singapore does not produce all its exports but re-exports additional species, which are collected or reared in other Asian countries. Singapore is a duty free zone, so there are no heavy imports to pay. It exports to more than 60 countries around the world, including Japan, USA, UK, Germany, France, Italy, Spain, the Netherlands and Australia.

The second largest exporter was Malaysia with exports valued at US$ 14.37 million, 7.9 per cent of exports. This was followed by Indonesia (US$ 13.72 million, 7.5 per cent) Czech Republic (US$ 11.27 million, or 6.2 per cent) and Peru (US$ 9.78 million, 5.4 per cent). China came next with total exports of US$ 11 million. China's exports were mainly through its special Administrative Region of Hong Kong, which also serves as a trading center. Hong Kong's exports amounted to US$ 8.97 million. This was followed by Japan (US$ 7.69 million, 4.2 per cent), USA (US$ 7.05 million, 3.9 per cent), the Philippines (US$ 6.50 million, 36 per cent) and Sri Lanka (US$ 5.94 million, 3.3 per cent).

Asia is by far the biggest exporter contributing 59.1 per cent of world exports or US$ 107.96 million in 2001. The other regions which export in significant quantities are Europe (20.6 per cent, US$ 37.68 million), South America (10.0 per cent, US$ 18.34 million), North America (3.9 per cent, US$ 7.06 million) an the Middle East (3.2 per cent, US$ 5.81 million). The major Asian countries involved in the export of ornamental fish are Singapore (38.5 per cent of Asian supplies), Malaysia (13.3 per cent), Indonesia (12.7 per cent), China including Hong Kong and Macau (10.2 per cent), Japan (7.1 per cent), the Philippines (6.0 per cent), Sri Lanka (5.5 per cent), Thailand (3.1 per cent), Taiwan (1.6 per cent) and India (1.2 per cent).

The Demand Situation

Total world imports of ornamental fish rose from US$ 216.327 million in 1991 to a peak of US$ 5337.625 million in 1994. Thereafter, imports declined gradually to US$ 244.097 million in 1999, raising slightly to US$ 246.161 million in 2000 and finishing off at US$ 244.618 million in 2001.

Fish keeping is a hobby, which is practiced mainly in the industrialized countries. Consequently, the main importers of ornamental fish are USA, Japan and countries in Western Europe. Total world imports of ornamental fish in 2001 were valued at US$ 244.62 million. The top importer was the USA with US$ 61.77 million worth of imports equivalent to 25.3 per cent of total imports. This was followed by Japan with US$ 528.40 million or 11.6 per cent of total imports. The other major importing countries were Germany (US$ 21.09 million; 8.6 per cent), UK (US$ 21.09 million; 8.6 per cent), France (US$ 20.56 million; 8.4 per cent), Singapore (US$ 9.93 million; 4.1 per cent), Belgium (US$ 9.45 million; 3.9 per cent), Italy (US$ 9.07 million; 3.7 per cent), the Netherlands (US$ 8.16 million; 3.3 per cent), China/Hong Kong (3.1 per cent) and Canada (2.7 per cent). Both Singapore and Hong Kong, being important trading hubs, re-export a major portion of their imports.

The US Market

The USA is the world's largest single market for ornamental fish. Its imports declined in value from US$ 77.860 million in 1996 to a low of US$ 57 359 million in 1999, and then rose again from 2000 to a figure of US$ 61.766 million in 2001. With about 10 per cent of households possessing aquaria, the country is estimated to have more than 10 million home aquaria. Some 40 per cent of the households with aquaria have more than one aquarium. The imports are mainly of freshwater species. With two species the guppy and the neon tetra accounting for 40 per cent of the market. Some of the other popular species are mollies, swordtails, goldfish, discus, angelfish, African cichlids, zebra danios and platies. The major suppliers to the US market are Singapore, Thailand, Indonesia, Philippines, Malaysia and Brazil.

The Japanese Market

Japan is the second largest single market. The growing prohibitions on keeping animal pets such a cats and dogs in high-rise apartments has given a boost to the aquariums becoming an important feature of the home décor. The country is estimated to have some 1.2 million aquarists. The most popular species are guppy (28 per cent of the market), neon tetra, red nose tetra, cardinal tetra, black tetra, tiger barb, harlequin fish, discus, angelfish. Siamese fighting fish, gourami, platy, swordtail, julli catfish (corydoras), algae eater, white clouds and Zebra danio. Imports fell in value gradually from US$ 73.94 million in 1996 to US$ 28.398 million in 2001. The decline has been attributed mainly to the recession the country has been going through. The main suppliers to the Japanese market are Singapore, Brazil, Indonesia, Malaysia, USA and China (Hong Kong).

The Western Europe Market

Western Europe is the largest trade block. It imports almost 40 per cent of world ornamental fish production. Freshwater species account for more than 90 per cent of imports by value, the rest being marine fish, invertebrates and live rocks. Among the most popular species are neon tetra, cardinal tetra, guppy, platy, swordtail. Siamese fighting fish, angelfish, corydoras, rasbora, gouramy and loach. Imports fell from US$ 123.226 million in 1996 to US$ 107.217 million in 2000 rising slightly to US$ 107.767 million in 2001. The major suppliers to this market are Singapore the Czech Republic Israel and Japan. The top importing countries in 2001 were Germany (21.0 per cent), UK (19.6 per cent), France (19.1 per cent), Belgium (8.8 per cent), Italy (8.4 per cent) and the Netherlands (7.6 per cent).

The main suppliers to the Western Europe market are Singapore, Czech Republic, Israel, Japan, Malaysia, Indonesia, China (Hong Kong), Sri Lanka, Thailand, USA and Brazil.

Indian Scenario

India, despite its vast area of sea coast and flow of perennial rivers and consequent abundant resources of freshwater and marine ornamentals, is still way behind other developing countries in the matter of development of this trade. In fact, the natural resources of India are more varied as compared to those of Sri Lanka, Africa, Singapore, Indonesia and Malaysia. Several freshwater varieties of Indian fishes are well known in the international market. The lagoons and coral reefs of lakshadweep and Minicoy Islands. Andaman and Nicobar Islands, Gulf of Kutch complex, coast of Kerala around Cape Comorin, Gulf of Mannar and Palk Bay around with highly attractive and varied species of ornamental fishes. We could certainly makes a good deal of money and enjoy a considerable share in the world trade by supplying marine ornamental fishes and live rocks originating from the vast resources which are the basic material essential in keeping the aquarium environment healthy. Live rocks afford organisms living in it a much longer life span. Poor knowledge on the part of our people about aquariculture and live fish trade could be the principal reason for our backwardness in this field.

India's contribution to global aquarium trade is worth of Rs. 5.7 crores, 0.5 per cent of international trade in 2005-06 while we have a great potential to increase the level of exports to about US$ 30 million (about Rs. 110 crores) every year.

Economics of Simple Backyard Goldfish Culture Unit

a. Non-Recurring

1. Cement tanks		
2 x 1.5 x 0.7m	- 5 Nos. @ Rs. 500/-	= Rs. 2500
1 x 0.6 x 0.4m	- 5 Nos. @ Rs. 200/-	= Rs. 1000
2. Glass tanks		
45 x 20 x 30cm	- 10 Nos. @ Rs. 250/-	= Rs. 2500
3. Motor pump (0.5 HP)	- 1 No.	= Rs. 2000
4. Aerators	- 4 Nos. @ Rs. 250/-	= Rs. 1000
	Total (A)	= Rs. 9000

b. Recurring

1. Cost of Gold fish (brood fishes) 10 pairs		= Rs. 2000
2. Farm implement (Net, bucket, etc.)		= Rs. 1000
3. Feed and Medicine		= Rs. 9000
	Total (B)	= Rs. 12,000

c. Income

Expected annual income by sale after 3 months

1. Gold fish (15,000 Nos.) @ Rs. 5/fish		= Rs. 75,000
	Total income	= Rs. 75,000

Total Expenditure

Interest on Capital	= Rs. 1,350
Recurring Cost	= Rs. 12,000
Total	= Rs. 13,350

Net Income = Rs. 75,000–Rs. 13,350 = Rs. 61,650/-

References

Ahilan, B., 1996. Technology development for mass culture of goldfish *Carassius auratus* (Linnaeus) through induced maturation and spawning. Un pub. *Ph.D., Thesis*, Fisheries College & Research Institute, TANUVAS, Thoothukudi, p. 183.

Ahilan, B,, Felix, N. and Santhanam, R., 2008. *Textbook of Aquariculture*. Daya Publishing House, New Delhi, p. 157.

Aexlrod, H.R. and Schultz, P.L., 1983. *Handbook of Tropical Aquarium Fishes*. T.F.H. Publications, Hong Kong, p. 28-30.

Bhat, B.V., 2008. Export oriented aquaculture in India: An overview. *Fishing Chimes*, 27 (10/11): 51-58.

Boyd, C.E., 1992. *Water Quality Management for Pond Fish Culture*. Elsevier Science Publishers, Netherland, p. 317.

Dey, V.K., 1993. *Ornamental Fishes*. Marine Products Export Development Authority, Kochi. pp. 7-10.

Dey, V.K., 2008. Global Trade in Ornamental Fish: Trends, Prospects and Issues. *Abstract*, International seminar on Ornamental fish breeding, farming and trade, Cochin, India, pp. 2.

FAO, 2007. *Fishery Statistics, Aquaculture Production, 2005.* Food and Agriculture Organization of the United Nations, Rome.

Harris, J.C., 1987. *Goldfish*. T.F.H. Publications, U.S.A., pp. 4-11.

Hervey, G.F. and Hems, J., 1968. *The Goldfish.* Faber and Faber Limited, Great Britain, pp. 265.

Joseph Smart . 2001. *Goldfish: Varieties and Genetics*. Fishing News Books, USA, p. 216.

Lochmann, R.T. and Phillips, H., 1994. Dietry protein requirement of golden shiners (*Notemigonus crysoleucas*) and goldfish (*Carassius auratus*) in aquaria. *Aquaculture,* 128: 277-285.

Moyle, P.B. and Cech, J.J., 1988. *Fishes: An Introduction to Ichthyology*, 2nd edition, Prentice Hall, Englewood Cliffs, NJ.

MPEDA, 2000. *Statistics of Marine Products Exports, 2000.* MPEDA, India, p. 25.

Petrovicky, I., 1993. *Tropical Aquarium Fishes*. Chancellor Press, London, p. 258.

Purdom, C.M., 1993. *Genetics and Fish Breeding*. Chapman and Hall, London, p. 277.

Ramachandran, A., 1999. International Trade in Ornamental Fish. *12th Indian Seafood Trade Fair, Souvenir*. Seafood Exporters Association, India, pp.24-29.

Santhanam, R., Sukumaran, N. and Natarajan, P., 1990. *A Manual of Freshwater Aquaculture*. Oxford & IBH Publishing Co. Pvt. Ltd., New Delhi, p. 102-120.

Shinji Mekino, 1972. *Home Aquarium, Aquatic Gems: Tropical Fish*. Ward Lock Limited, London, p. 97.

Singh, T. and Dey, V.K., 2003. Ornamental fish trade runs into billions. *Info Fish Int.*, 5: 54-60.

Thomas, K., 2008. Status of Ornamental fish trade in India with special reference to investment and trade opportunities. *Abstract, International Seminar on Ornamental Fish Breeding, Farming and Trade*, Cochin, India, pp. 7.

Wainwright, N., 1969. *Coldwater Aquarium*. Frederick Warne & Co. Ltd., England, p. 75.

Index